Becoming A Pioneer

Becoming A Pioneer

A Book Series

The Month-by-Month Guide
to Doubling Your Business and
Taking Over Your industry in a Year

Bimal shah

Book 3: Eliminating Your Biggest Dangers and Obstacles

Becoming a Pioneer - Book 3
© Copyright 2022 by Bimal Shah

ISBN: 978-1-0880-7702-3 Paperback

ISBN: 978-0-9909014-4-0 Hard Cover

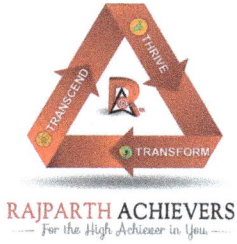

RAJPARTH **ACHIEVERS**
— For the High Achiever in You. —

TheOneYearBreakthrough.com

For more information, email: Bimal@theoneyearbreakthrough.com

Rajparth Achievers, LLC
5550 Glades Road, Suite 500
Boca Raton, FL 33431

Connect with Pioneers around the World. Every Month. With the book purchase, you are a member. No strings attached.

Join Me and walk away with personalized insights for you in the monthly club meeting.

Get Your Free Membership here:
https://bit.ly/ThePioneersClub

Learn Exponentially More

This book is best used in conjunction with this training, which allows you to not only eliminate your biggest danger or overcome your biggest obstacles but also make a big leap in your business goals.

Get Your Free Video Training at
https://bit.ly/TheDangerEliminator

To my wife, Ami, and our daughters, Rajvi and Parthvi. This book would not have been possible without the efforts of my wife, Ami, with the editing. Her strength and support are priceless. Also, I am indebted to my daughters for invaluable insight on structure and design. My family is everything to me.

I love them with all my heart.

Content

Author's Preface

Making Pioneers! —The What and Why

What is a Pioneer?

A pioneer is unique and different from the rest.

To be a pioneer, you need to be the Only One at something. This book is about breaking all the barriers and obstacles you have in your life, work, habits, and mindset. The purpose is to bring a 10x to a 100x transformation in your perspective about your own self—to assist you in realizing your true potential in a very short time.

Why be a Pioneer?

God has made every human being unique. When every human becomes unique, the whole world can work in harmony. Becoming a pioneer happens through stages and discoveries. I wrote this book with the intent to create a map to the essential stages and discoveries you will need at each step. Drawing from my own experiences, it builds fresh perspectives that can take your business to the next level.

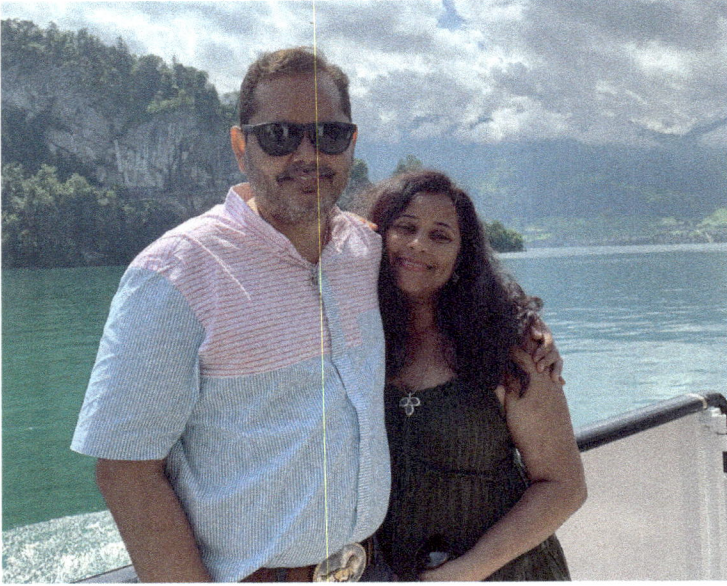

Editor Ami Shah with Author Bimal Shah

Introduction

How to Get the Most Out of This Book Series

Go slow. You do not want to read this book fast. Write in the book. Scribble in it, make notes, have sticky notes with you. Carry this book with you wherever you go. This is your book and customized manual to help you at least double what you believe you can do in a year.

Even if you answer one question from this book, it will have a positive impact in your life or business. Below are five ways you can make the most out of it:

1. Read first, think second, and then write: Read a sentence or two or a paragraph. Think about it and answer the questions that follow.

2. Go digging: Look up something in your business or your life related to the question. And then come back and answer the question.

3. Use Sharp Pencils with an eraser on top: instead of using pens, please use pencils, as the answers may change in due course while you are writing your thoughts on the questions.

4. Watch the video before you start reading: in the video, you will get a lot more insights about the book itself. It will walk you through powerful elements to scale.

5. Scan the QR CODE and save the QR CODE link in your notes on your Smartphone: When you answer a specific question, look up the links listed in the Link Tree. See if there is a resource for the problem you are trying to solve. The Link Tree is very useful. It works like magic; you will find new and amazing things each time you look.

Special Advice for Using This Book in Uncertain

Economic Times

As we all know, the future is in question. To stabilize and speed up your income growth, I recommend using this book series in a sequential order. Follow the advice in the acronym UNCERTAIN:

U - Unique - Discover from each book how to become unique.
Book #5 lists elements to leverage to be unique.

N - New – Apply the different tools and systems taught in book #1, book #9, and book #11. To bring in the new you in record time.

C -Confident – Use the Confidence Journey tool from book #5. To build daily confidence in your journey.

E - Empathetic – Use the Self-Empathy skills from books #10 and #2 (this one). To deal with uncertainties, biggest pains, or frustrations.

R - Resilient – Lay the foundation for building resilience with a powerful vision in book #1. Apply the book #12 resiliency skills.

T - Transparent – Discover from books #3, #4, and #6 how to use good or bad transparency. This is about you and your business, to propel to the next level.

A - Audacious –From book #1, book #13, and book #6 you will discover how to maintain and chase audacious goals.

I - Implementation – From book #7 on Sprints and book #8 on Leadership. Throughout each book in the series, you will become a master implementor. Leaders lead by example.

N - Next Steps – Every single chapter in each book helps you build your customized next steps. There is no way you can't stabilize or grow if you follow all the steps you built by yourself using this book series.

How to use this Book Series in Prosperous Economic Times.

When times are good, you can make them better by using this book series with the acronym AWESOME as follows:

A - <u>Algorithms</u> - In business when there are a lot of opportunities coming your way, you need to apply an algorithm: a one-line business plan. Build your customized scale from algorithms listed in book #4 and book #13.

W - <u>Wins</u> – At the end of every chapter, you celebrate your wins. In book #5 you have the tools that make it a recurring habit.

E - <u>Extra</u> Mile –In book #12, you will have the systems to drive on the no-traffic roads. There is no traffic riding beside you in the extra mile.

S - <u>Surprisers</u> –What to do when your team and customers surprise you. You are bound to get surprised quite often. Discover best responses in books #1, #2 (this book), #3, #4, and #10.

O - <u>Omnipresence</u> –Through book #6 and book #3, you will build your own systems. Through book #11 you will build your own skill sets. Through book #9 you will build the platforms. In book #10 you will have the systems and tools to automate omnipresence.

M - <u>Multiplication</u> –When times are good, you need systems to multiply. Through book #1 you will lay the foundation for multiplication. Through book #7 you will build the skills. Through books #8 and #9 you will build the traits for becoming a multiplier and the systems essential for it.

E - <u>Extinguishers</u> –When things are happening in rapid fire, you will need a different kind of extinguisher. This is to extinguish the fires and sustain the pace you are moving at. Build your own fire extinguishers from book #3.

Introduction

Becoming a Pioneer was written with the intent to make an immediate positive impact on you, the reader.

Hence, there are a lot of questions, with valuable tools, resources, stories, and action steps.

This way, when you answer even one question, you can see a positive impact.

I want you to make your notes from this book. And that's why there is a lot of space for you. I have noticed many people have larger handwriting and need more space to write!

I want you to make this your **"own unique book."**

There are many self-development and business books out there. But I wrote this one to direct your thinking in a specific way. So, sit back and relax while you read.

There is one topic in this book that allows you to go deep. It also helps to make a real positive difference in the least amount of time.
Even if you spend five minutes reading this book, you will feel the transformation.

What's unique and different is that it is a series you will cherish forever.

It has your goals, your plans, your actions, and most of all a system you can use every year.

The system consists of a series of 13 stages. Each one lasts 4 Weeks; you can achieve your 3-year goal in a single Year.

There are important questions for you to answer, tools for you to use. And some practical solutions you can put in place and see great results.

I hope this book will make a very positive impact on your life.

I look forward to meeting you in Part IV!

Week 1

Obstacles Are a Blessing in Disguise

I used to think obstacles make the journey so difficult, make you get stuck or go in reverse. But now, I know to welcome them and think of them as blessings in disguise.

My better half once told me when something good happens, it is God looking out for you. And when something bad happens, it is also God looking out for your benefit.

You may not realize it now, but you will when the time is right. That's when I started wondering, as most of us have our religion of faith, how does God teach us or help us?

The easiest way for God to make us better and stronger in our path is to put obstacles in our way and help us find our direction.

Another recent true story about the Iron man of Business, Elon Musk:

In the third quarter of 2021, almost every company in the car industry was plummeting in sales. The reason was, they couldn't get the necessary microchips and labor. But Elon had the best quarter ever in history. How? Why? He believed in his and his team's ability to figure things out. They figured out how to modify the microchip. If they didn't know how, they learned. They built the new algorithm, and they made it happen.

Below in this book, I would like to walk you through a series of questions. I will show you the next steps, tools, and exercises that will help you. They will prepare you on how to "welcome obstacles and hurdles in your life and business."

What is the biggest goal you want to achieve in your business?

_____
_____
_____
_____

Yes, I always emphasize the word "biggest." Why? Overcoming your biggest obstacle and dangers will produce the greatest impact in your life.

It will provide the direction you want for your life and business. According to the Pareto Principle, 80 percent of consequences stem from 20 percent of causes.

Dangers are the things that push us backward instead of forwards. Instead of making progress, we are stuck in the same place we were before. It could also mean that you are moving forward or backward at a slow pace.

Now let's identify your biggest danger.

What is your biggest danger, the one standing in the way of your biggest goal?

_____
_____
_____
_____

Is your above answer truly your biggest danger? ☐ Y ☐ N

If yes, then congratulations. Let's get to work helping you overcome it. If no, please go back, ponder hard and identify your biggest danger. To help you find the answer, try to answer the questions below honestly. After you have done so, you will be able to identify your biggest danger truly.

Imagine it is three years from today and that your biggest goal in business has come true. What does your business look like?

_____
_____
_____
_____

What do you imagine your life to be like?

_____
_____
_____
_____

Let yourself go wild: think of your wildest dreams, your greatest imagination.

Now, think of what could be holding you back. What is your greatest fear? What could happen to prevent you from achieving what you desire?

_____
_____
_____
_____

What are you scared of that might hurt your success?

_____
_____
_____
_____

Fear is good for you. Think of fear as caution. So, what precautions do you need? How can avoid getting into dangers that can crush you or push you back to a great extent? That's it. Think about the above questions.

At the end of your thought process, you will have identified your biggest danger. You will see what is preventing you from living the life you want. Thumbs up on identifying it. Now let's get to work on helping you achieve the life and business you deserve.

If you overcome the danger, you stated above, would it give you a major boost towards achieving your three-year goal in the next 90 days? ☐ Y ☐ N

If yes, you are on the right track, and we can now talk about your biggest obstacle. If no, please go back and ponder what truly might be your biggest danger.

Obstacles are different from dangers. They are things or elements that you encounter while moving forward. And you must overcome them to move forward. Obstacles are the raw materials for all great progress. Now, let's identify your biggest obstacle.

What is your biggest obstacle?

_____
_____
_____
_____

Is your answer truly your biggest obstacle? ☐ Y ☐ N

If yes, then well done! You have made significant progress toward achieving your goals. If not, we need to identify your biggest obstacle. If you eliminate obstacles from your business, it will give you smooth sailing in all aspects of it.

What do you think is holding your business back from achieving the success you seek?

_____
_____
_____
_____

From research, perspective is the biggest obstacle anyone can ever overcome. We can tell ourselves lies about why we are not achieving our dreams. We must learn to be truthful to ourselves. Else, either in our lives or in our businesses we are our own stumbling blocks on the road to success.

What are some of the lies you have told yourself that are holding your business back?

_____

Yes, we call them lies because they are not true. We tell ourselves these lies to comfort ourselves. We do not want to feel bad about failing. Michelle Obama put it quite nicely, when she said, step out of your comfort zone and soar.

Knowing what you know now, what are the things that are holding you back from doing your best in your business?

What is blocking your success? What is keeping you at a standstill? What is making you not grow in your place of work and life?

Think about these things, and honestly identify your biggest obstacle.

An obstacle is not a risk or an issue; it is something that prevents you from effectively doing what you are supposed to do. Simply say, "An obstacle is a detriment to my success."
What would be your ideal business if you didn't have any biggest obstacle hindering your growth?

Now that we have successfully identified your biggest obstacle, what differences will occur in your business if you eliminate these obstacles?

_____

_____

_____

_____

Once you can visualize your business opportunities and expansion better, you will then be able to come up with ways to get rid of the obstacles quickly.

Name 5 steps you need to take to remove your biggest obstacle from your path to success. When you identify these steps, write the sentences in the format of *who needs to do what by when* to achieve an end goal.

Example: "I want to build $120,000 in reserves in a year. So, what can I do? I need to save $10,000 from my business operating account into my reserve account at the end of every month."

1._____
_____

2._____
_____

3._____
_____

4._____
_____

5._____
_____

Both dangers and obstacles are impairments to success. The words may be used interchangeably, but there are some differences that are worthy of note. And the differences are given below:

Danger	Obstacle
This is the possibility that something bad or harmful will happen. It implies something unpleasant that you may encounter. Also, danger can mean a liability to all kinds of long-term consequences or injuries that is imminent or remote. Example of a danger with long-term consequences: you may think habitually over-billing your customers will allow you to make a lot of money, but then one day, when there is a legal investigation and consequence, your business suffers irreparable damages. You could have risks that are difficult to repair or come out of that completely change the direction of your life or business. Whatever the danger is, you need to eliminate it or step away from it, as it will completely change the path or course of your life.	This is something that obstructs or hinders your progress. It interferes with or prevents your growth. An obstacle can be material or non-material. Example of a material obstacle to your progress: someone is delaying the renovation plans for your new office space. Example of a nonmaterial obstacle: your mind is telling you that you are okay, and you shouldn't aim for more because you won't get it, so you should be content to live a mediocre life. Your obstacles are like raw materials for your success, and you want to use them to build systems or solutions that improve your life or your business for the long term. Whatever the obstacle is, you need to overcome it, as it will prevent you from owning the life of your dreams.

Below is an illustration on how to use dangers and obstacles for doubling your business or even reaching exponential growth.

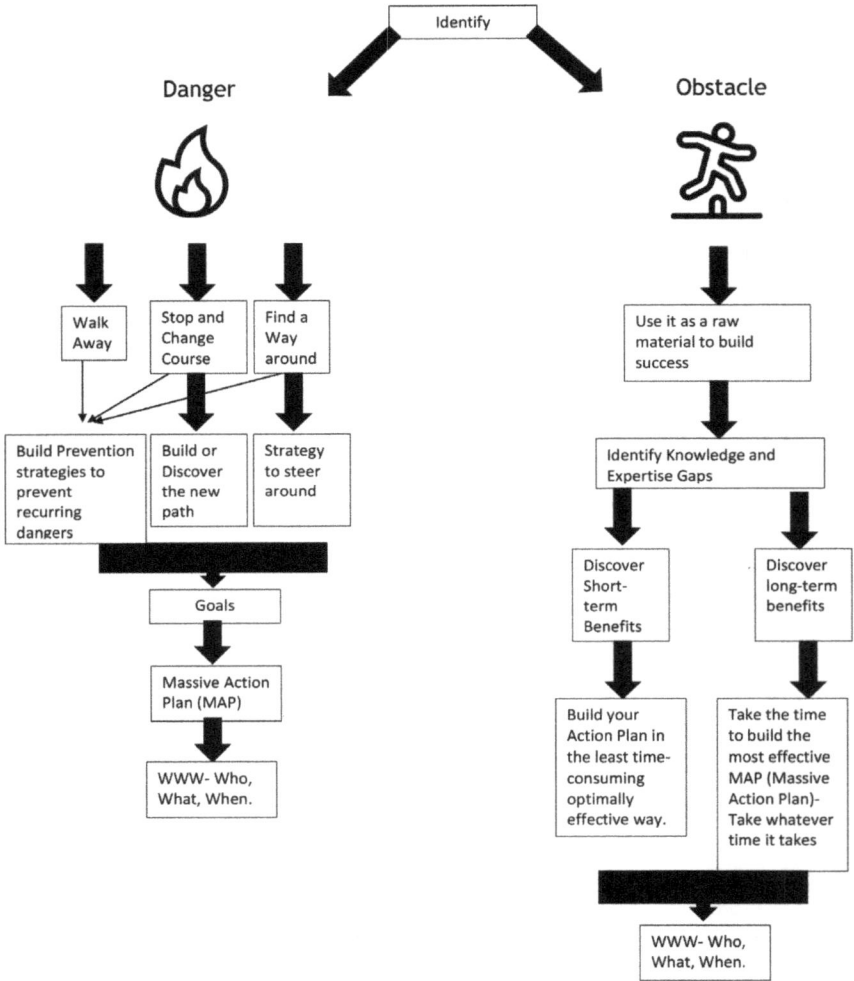

Ability to predict danger can be profitable to your business. It shows you are forward-thinking and possess foresight. Apart from identifying danger, you need to be able to plot a path to avoid it.

Identify the top 5 dangers to your business.

1._____

_____

2._____

_____

3._____

_____

4._____

_____

5._____

_____

You can prevent these dangers from occurring. And if they have happened because of certain events, decisions, habits, or situations that have occurred in the past, identify these situations, events, decisions, and habits. They can help you find a way of preventing these dangers from occurring again.

List 5 ways you can avoid these dangers.

1._____

_____

2._____

_____

3._____

_____

4._____

_____

5._____

_____

When starting a business, your major focus is on all the positives. It is understandable because, truth be told, if you are not thinking of the positive aspect and gains the business will bring, why start it in the first place?

What made you decide to start your business?

_____

_____

_____

_____

But there will be a time when you must think of the not-so-rosy side of a business, the dangers, and the risks.

For a fact, I know that the risk and dangers present in any business is quite as long as the list of the benefits. But this should not deter you, as those dangers do not have to get in the way of running a successful business. The solution is knowing how to foresee these dangers to prevent them and if they occur deal with them.

What are the top 5 dangers you foresee to your business success?

1._____

_____

2._____

_____

3._____

_____

4._____

_____

5._____

_____

Every business owner starts a business with the mind of achieving exponential growth. Only a small percentage reach the growth they desire. In 2019, the failure rate of startups was 90 percent. And research has concluded that 21.5 percent of startups fail in their first year, while 30 percent fail in the second year, and 50 percent in their fifth year. And in the tenth year, a full 70 percent fail.[1] This is because there are so many barriers to growth. And most business owners struggle to grow. Thus, struggle to identify areas or factors that can become obstacles in the future. So, you can plan on how to overcome these obstacles.

If you don't overcome your obstacles as and when they happen, they become barriers. Consider babies growing into toddlers, then into teenagers, then adults. Barriers are more difficult to overcome than obstacles. Barriers need some significant shifts that are often very hard to bring about. But they are necessary in order to make progress.

What are the top 5 barriers to your business growth?

1._____
_____
2._____
_____
3._____
_____
4._____
_____
5._____
_____

How do you plan to overcome these barriers to your business success, or who do you need to get help from to overcome these barriers?

_____
_____
_____
_____

Barriers seem like a problem. Problems often are puzzle pieces, and you need to identify all the pieces to the puzzle so you can solve it. When you say to yourself, "I need to solve this problem," you are essentially saying you need to solve a puzzle. To solve the puzzle requires identifying all the pieces. You need to ask yourself questions to know what they are, then develop a plan to put them together. One of the most important pieces of that puzzle is your mindset.

Is your mindset holding your business back? ☐ Y ☐ N

A negative mindset will hurt your business. If you have a negative mindset, you must think differently and be positive in your thoughts and actions. It will enhance your business growth. Research says a positive mindset is key to increased performance in the workplace.

What are the 5 steps you can take to work on your mindset? How can you start thinking positively about your business growth?

1._____
_____
2._____
_____
3._____
_____
4._____
_____
5._____
_____

"Growth mindset" in your business happens by working on the business. Are you taking more than half or even 80 percent of your time working "in" rather than "on" your business? ☐ Y ☐ N

If you answered yes, then that itself is a major barrier, and you need to shift your time to working on the business as much as you can. If no, then that's great, and you are working on growth strategies for your business.

This question seeks to probe your mind so you will know if you have gotten sidetracked by the day- to-day running of your business. Or perhaps you have forgotten to focus on your strategy and growth. You must devote time to business development and strategy to grow the way you envision it. This is the aspect of the business called research and development. It is vital for business growth.
Do you have a research and development team? ☐ Y ☐ N

If yes, that's great. The next step is to make sure they deliver consistent and trackable results. If no, you can start building your team at https://bit.ly/MyDreamEmployee.

What 5 steps can you take to work on your business development and strategy?

1._____
_____
2._____
_____
3._____
_____
4._____
_____
5._____
_____

Do you have the required knowledge, skills, and experience to run your business? ☐ Y ☐ N

If yes, think about how you can improve them. If no, think about where and how you can acquire them.

This question applies to you and your team members. If anyone is lacking in an aspect, consider investing in increasing your knowledge. Also invest in your team members, so you all can work at optimal levels to effectively grow your business.

Who needs to do what by when to fill the knowledge gap in yourself or your teammates?

1._____
_____
2._____
_____
3._____
_____
4._____
_____
5._____
_____

Also, make a list of who needs to increase their knowledge, in what area and when; create a timeline for them to upskill.

Who	Knowledge gap	Timeline to upskill

As a business owner, do not shy away from the risks, dangers, and obstacles involved in running a business. Otherwise, it will destroy your business. And it might be too late to control the damage. Prevention is always the better option.

Knowing what you know now, do you shy away from dangers and obstacles? ☐ Y ☐ N

If yes, you have a mindset issue. If no, you are ready to take actions and move forward.

What 5 steps will you take when you catch yourself running away from dangers and obstacles?

1._____

_____

2._____

_____

3._____

_____

4._____

_____

5._____

_____

Name the obstacles you see coming your way. A business owner does always face them. You don't have to run away from them; you need checklists. Scorecards are one of the most measurable tools for business. Your business scorecard is a very valuable resource.

How do measure each function in your business? Define it in your own words.

A scorecard is a business tool. It shows organizations a snapshot of their current performance. It helps in comparison to goals. It makes it easier for business owners and organizations to manage their performances. And allows them to make better, more well-informed strategic decisions.

Will you use the business scorecard in your organization? ☐ Y ☐ N

What do you think scorecards can be used for?

1._____

2._____

3._____

4._____

5._____

Most businesses use scorecards to track their Key Performance Indicators (KPI). They focus on the current tracked value and the targeted value. One major advantage of the business scorecards is, they serve to track the strategic goals of your business in relation to your KPIs. And they help you make decisions on a much bigger scale.

What are the top 5 key performance indicators of your business that need to be tracked?

1._____
_____

2._____
_____

3._____
_____

4._____
_____

5._____
_____

Some of the decisions include measuring the efficiency of individual departments towards meeting set goals, tracking the progress of a given strategy, or even helping to identify dangers and how they can be resolved.

Would you use a weekly or monthly business scorecard? Why?
_____
_____
_____
_____

Scorecards are periodic measurements. They are updated at set intervals, weekly or monthly. Think about the best periodic interval. Which one would need to have your business scorecard updated?

In the next page, I will provide The Business Scorecard with instructions on how to use it. I have developed it for you so you can score your business. Also, discover the gaps in your business and apply the information to your future goals. How to fill them, and what would be the financial impact of the same if you did it.

The Business Scorecard™

Your Name: _____ Cell Phone: _____ Email: _____
Your Current Score (A) _____ Where do you want your score to be ? (B): _____ : Today's Date _____ Date of Y

Business Functions	I am Unhappy			I am Frustrated			I am winning on certain fronts		
	1	2	3	4	5	6	7	8	
Marketing	You get more revenue from the same market improving the same methods. It usually takes you an unpredictable amount of time and effort to transform prospects into customers. Your customers have a satisfying experience.			You try different markets and focus your marketing on whatever is trending right now. You are constantly frustrated with the inconsistency in results from marketing. You just focus on top of mind awareness advertising.			You have narrowed down markets but still overwhelming. Fe of your marketing efforts are really paying off 5X or higher. You are able to get great reviews from some of your customers.		
Operations	You are able to get things done if you stay on top of your team. You have some parts of your operations functioning well on their own. You believe the forces outside your control limit your capabilities to improve your operations in the company.			A portion of your team gives you the results you want without your intervention, but many can't. You are continually changing course to see what sticks frustrating yourself and others. You are losing more than acceptable number of customers to competition.			You only have a few painful team members or departments in you company. You have key people running operations well but can improve significantly. You are able to improve processes on a monthly basis.		
Sales	Your business is growing between 10-25 percent a year. You have a lot of fat and very little muscle in your sales team. Your sales closing ratio is 30 percent or below.			You are growing more than 25 percent but your profit margins are down. Your growth is also increasing the inefficiencies in other areas. You are scaling but feel sacrificing quality.			You are growing more than 50 percent a year. You are able t manage your growth by working long hours and staying on top. You are able to maintain quality but not improve it.		
Training and Development	You and your team are learning and improving but inconsistently. You have invested in coaching irregularly because you haven't seen satisfactory results. Your team is doing better, believes in maintaining what you have, and holding on to what you have achieved so far.			You have some consistency in your training. You have invested in coaching but hasn't got you to where you want to. You are trying new initiatives but not getting the expected results out of it.			Half of your team have taken initiative and training on their own or have become leaders to train others. You have invested in specialized coaching that has paid off but lack at many other areas in the business. You have a systematic way of approaching new initiatives but not scaling		
Innovation	You start many things but they never take off. You change a few things from what you hear from non-credible sources but haven't seen satisfactory results. You have successfully implemented a few ideas that have paid off satisfactory results.			You procrastinate and can't take initiatives to a finish line. With the fast paced changes, you feel you should maintain course by implementing essential changes until bought out or eliminated. You have a team that you delegate ideas but they are consistently stuck in 'Work-In-Progress'			You have implemented a good number of ideas successfully. You have developed systems to evaluate new ideas, but requires a lot of improvement. You are consistently innovative but not seeing the traction you want to see.		
Human Relations (HR-Employees)	You handle majority of the decisions when it comes to hiring, raising, terminating employees. Your team is performing satisfactory results but can be a whole lot better. You have to consistently involved in HR for it to run function well and this is draining energy, time and resources that you could devote elsewhere.			You have successfully delegated the decision making but often discover late in the game that HR was waiting for directions or permission from you. Your Gross Profit is 3 times payroll or lower. You have to dedicate some time every week to HR to see it function well.			Half of your team is functioning well on their own. You are driving towards a result based culture but aren't there yet. Your gross profit is between 3-5 times payroll.		
Technology	You have technology that supports and maintains your business but doesn't grow it. You feel investment in technology is a necessary evil and are doing it without clear measurables. Your technology is creating measurable improvements in certain areas of the business			Your technology is growing certain areas of the business and improving efficiencies. Your measurables are there and giving certain improvements but overall growth is not there–making you frustrated. You have a technology person or team in house who can be greatly improved.			You are proud of some of the technology you have as your business and how it has helped grow Top Line revenue. You are consistently experimenting for next-level growth using technology but haven't quite fou it. Your technology is helping you grow up to 50 percent a year in the business		
Customer Advocacy	The number of customers getting frustrated with the processes, people, and mistakes is on the rise. You have an acceptable customer dissatisfaction rate. You have good reviews for your services but not enough.			You are able to make your customers happy by offering them discounts or refunds. You are slightly improving your customer happiness rate. Your customers would easily switch to competitors for a lower price.			You are making customers happy by providing a great experience but its n consistent. You have a few really good raving fans. Your customers won't switch to competitors as long as you provide the exceptional service–but th needs improvement in many areas.		
Finances-Numbers	You are improving some of the numbers in your P&L but not all. You don't know what's the most important number you need to focus on. Your team is able to contribute in strategies to reduce expenses and grow the sales but can be greatly improved.			You are trying to improve the numbers but not getting any results. You can figure out what is the most important number to focus on for yourself but not for your team members. You are consistently increasing your expenses with as proportionate increases in revenues.			You are able to improve the essential numbers in your P&L Statemen You know what is the most important number for you and your key measures. You are able to get a satisfactory ROI on your expenses bu consistently looking for ways to scale the ROI on each line item.		
Head of Company	You wear too many hats and You are a slave to the business. You have a lot of help but overall you feel it's not dependable. You have unacceptable turnover and looking for replacements every quarter or sooner.			Your turnover has reduced. You are focused on wearing fewer hats but still overwhelmed. You have delegated majority of the tasks to be focused on your role as the CEO but can be greatly improved.			You are able to work 'ON' the business daily. You have a chronic way being super-productive at times but some quarters you are completely off track. You are able to take one or two long vacations with oversight and supervision while away.		
TOTAL	→			→			→		

The Business Scorecard™

Cell Phone: _____   Email: _____
A) _____ Where do you want your score to be ? (B): _____ : Today's Date _____ Date of Your Mastermind: _____

I am Frustrated	I am winning on certain fronts	I want to Transform	Your Score A	B
You try different markets and focus your marketing on whatever is trending right now. You are constantly frustrated with the inconsistency in results from marketing. You just focus on top of mind awareness advertising.	You have narrowed down markets but still overwhelming. Few of your marketing efforts are really paying off 5X or higher. You are able to get great reviews from some of your customers.	You want to predictably generate your required ideal customers every month for a known cost. You want to dominate a specific target market focused on the largest check' clientele. You want a system to consistently engage your ideal customers to increase revenues monthly.	2	12
A portion of your team gives you the results you want without your intervention, but many can't. You are continually changing course to see what sticks frustrating yourself and others. You are losing more than acceptable number of customers to competition.	You only have a few painful team members or departments in your company. You have key people running operations well but can improve significantly. You are able to improve processes on a monthly basis.	You want a well-oiled smooth running operations in my business at all times. You want a self-managing company. You want to take a sabatical and the company to run on its own	3	12
You are growing more than 25 percent but your profit margins are down. Your growth is also increasing the inefficiencies in other areas. You are scaling but feel sacrificing quality.	You are growing more than 50 percent a year. You are able to manage your growth by working long hours and staying on top. You are able to maintain quality but not improve it.	You want the shortest sales cycle in your industry. You want a system to consistently grow your sales exponentially. You want a predictable system that allows scaling but also has system to identify and fill the gaps to maintain the exponential scaling.	2	12
You have some consistency in your training. You have invested in coaching but hasn't got you to where you want to. You are trying new initiatives but not getting the expected results out of it.	Half of your team have taken initiative and training on their own or have become leaders to train others. You have invested in specialized coaching that has paid off but lack in many other areas in the business. You have a systematic way of approaching new initiatives but not scaling.	You want coaching and training that making scaling a systematic habit. You want to become the influential leader in your company and the industry. You want to automate training and development.	3	12
You procrastinate and can't take initiatives to a finish line. With the fast paced changes, you feel you should maintain course by implementing essential changes until bought out or eliminated. You have a team that you delegate ideas but they are consistently stuck in 'Work-In-Progress'.	You have implemented a good number of ideas successfully. You have developed systems to evaluate new ideas, but requires a lot of improvement. You are consistently innovating but not seeing the traction you want to see.	You want a system to bring great new ideas to fruition most effectively. You want to go from idea to execution in record time. You want to automate and systematize the 'new'.	2	12
You have successfully delegated the decision making but often discover late in the game that HR was waiting for directions or permission from you. Your Gross Profit is 3 times payroll or lower. You have to dedicate some time every week to HR to see it function well.	Half of your team is functioning well on their own. You are driving towards a result based culture but aren't there yet. Your gross profit is between 3-5 times payroll.	You want to have a team with exponential improvement consistently. You want to build a fail-proof hiring and retention system. You want your team to consistently deliver the results daily without your involvement.	2	12
Your technology is growing certain areas of the business and improving efficiencies. Your measurables are there and going certain improvements but overall growth is not there--making you frustrated. You have a technology person or team in house who can be greatly improved.	You are proud of some of the technology you have in your business and how it has helped grow Top Line revenue. You are consistently experimenting for next level growth using technology but haven't quite found it. Your technology is helping you grow up to 50 percent a year in the business.	You want adaptive technology that fuels exponential growth. You want technology that consistently brings automation, innovation, and optimization. You want technology that makes measurability in every aspect of your business a new norm.	3	12
You are able to make your customers happy by offering them discounts or refunds. You are slightly improving your customer happiness rate. Your competitors would easily switch to competitors as long as you provide the exceptional service for a lower price.	You are making customers happy by providing a great experience but its not consistent. You have a few really good raving fans. Your customers won't switch to competitors as long as you provide the exceptional service--but that needs improvement in many areas.	You want to make each of your customers a multiplier. Your customers make you omnipresent. You want a system to consistently exponentially scale the lifetime value of the customer.	2	12
You are trying to improve the numbers but not getting any results. You can figure out what is the most important number to focus on for yourself but not for your team members. You are consistently increasing your expenses with no proportionate increases in revenues	You are able to improve the essential numbers in your P&L Statement. You know what is the most important number for you and your key executives. You are able to get a satisfactory ROI on your expenses but consistently looking for ways to scale the ROI on each line item.	You want a system to consistently improve all numbers on your P&L. You want a financial algorithm for all possible line items in my P&L. You want a system to consistently scale your business value for a successful exit in the future.	2	12
Your turnover has reduced. You are focused on wearing fewer hats but still overwhelmed. You have delegated majority of the tasks to be focused on your role as the CEO but can be greatly improved.	You are able to work 'ON' the business daily. You have a chronic way of being super-productive at times but some quarters you are completely off track. You are able to take one or two long vacations with overnight and supervision while away.	You want to have an automated system of tracking your self-managing company. You want freedom of time, money, relationships and purpose. You want to have the right people in the right seats doing the right things all the time to get the right results for the right pay.	1	12
			24	120

The $ 100,000 or More Value

Your Name: _____ Cell Phone: _____

Your Current Score (A) _____ Where do you want your score to be ? (B): _____ : Tod

Business Functions	Your Score		Your Biggest Danger in the Way preventing The Score from where it needs to be?	Your Biggest Opportunities to get the score where it needs to be
	A	B		
Marketing	2	12	No clear strategy to get to $300 Million- Wasted Marketing	$2 Million each from 50 Mr. Cruiser, $100K each from 1000 Mrs. PA, and $20,000 from 5000 Mr. Importers
Operations	3	12	On the fly operations, missing A COO	Get A Dream Come True COO + CFO +CSO= "The Vision Executor"
Sales	2	12	I wear too many hats.	Free up 15 Hours Weekly for Sales in 90 Days
Training and Development	3	12	On the fly training that doesn't work	Effective SOP, Online Training University
Innovation	2	12	Improper Work-Flow, Constantly Putting Out Fires with Customers	Utilize All Systems and Tools of Bimal - The Process Innovator™ for all processes
Human Relations (HR-Employees)	2	12	Bad Hires, Need good Hiring and Retention Process, Bad employees cost millions, Putting Out Fires Daily- No time to hire	Turn-key Hiring System to hire and retain good employees, Employee Handbooks, The Confidence Scorer™
Technology	3	12	Very poor technology, I have to provide technical advise and be a trouble shooter many a time!!	Get Technology Platforms Identified, Innovative Processes,
Customer Advocacy	2	12	Daily 2-3 hours per Employee in Customer Callbacks and fixing problems, Costing $375,000 annually	Dream Come True Experience for The Customer
Finances- Numbers	2	12	Don't Understand how each expense contributes to Gross Profit and where to Focus	The DIDO Maximizer™ and Financial Algorithms
Head of Company	1	12	Horrible as CEO, Work 90 hours a week	Do only one thing- Right People in the Right Seats doing the Right Things
TOTAL	24	120		

e Results
_____ Email: _____
ay's Date _____ Total Value/Financial Impact: $ _____

Your Customized initial strategy to get to the score you want	Your Customized Initial Execution- Who Needs to do What by When?	Your Financial Gain/Value
Events Marketing, In-House Marketing Team, Vendor Registrations at 1000 Companies in the list, E-Commerce Platform	Targeted Marketing, 7 Touchpoints, Dedicated R&D Team, E-commerce Blueprint & Execution- 90 Days	$15,000,000
Hiring Process + The Process Innovator + The Operations Manual	Company Culture, Operations Manuals, SOPs, Checklists, & Reporting systems -90 Days	Priceless - $5,000,000
The Daily & Weekly Time Management System, The Sales Enigmatology™, Role Play Training, Sales Manuals	3 Workshops - 15 Hours Weekly Freed up, 3 Sales People hired and being trained in 90 Days.	$20,000,000
Essentials for Videos, Jason on SOPs and Quizzes,	Training University Launched with Top 20 Topics in 90 Days	Priceless
Automation at each step, Identify technology needed , Available Technology Partner, The Needle Shifter™	The Activity Analyzer™ - Eliminate and Delegate Activities for every employee and automation- 90 Days	Priceless - $5,000,000
Hiring System for Three hires in the next 60 days, Start The Confidence Scorer™	Handbooks- 30 days. Hiring process for three hires, Company Confidence Scoring	$2,500,000
Utilize Identified Platforms, The Process Innovator™, Technology patrners to build Customized Innovation	Team Conference, Training in the next 30 days, & Execute Customized Automation with a target time frame of 90 days.	$2,500,000
Dream Come True Experience Tool, Checklists, SOPs, and The Process Innovator™	The Dream Come True Experience Manual in 90 Days.	Priceless
The DIDO Questionnaire, Quickbooks Accountant Access, Work with in-house Comptroller for Reconciliation	Top 20 Action Items to Improve EBITDA - 90 Days	$1,500,000
Free up 40 Hours a week by end of the year	Agent book two vacations in next 12 months regardless in the next 10 days.	Priceless
	Total Financial Gain/ Value	$51,500,000

How to Use The Business Scorecard™

Outcome of the Tool: Give you an overall business Score of where you are and where you want to be to help create $100,000 or more in value for your business.

What is the Purpose of the Tool?
To discover every single element in your business that needs to be worked upon and create multiple strategies and executions that grows the business overall and not just one section of the business or company. That's what I created.

What to fill out?

You have to fill out the sections colored in light green in The Business Scorecard™ and The $100,000 Value Creator™. It is important to have these sections filled out and sent across three days before the date of your Mastermind. When you sent it across three days before, you will have the customized strategies and executions ready for you when you show up at the Mastermind that could add $100K or even millions to you in value for your business—All by filling it out, sending it across, and just showing up!!

This tool is best filled out when you are by yourself away from distractions or interruptions. If you don't know the answers to some of the functions, reach out to your team or key executives in the company and get them involved in the scorecard or get the answers.

What is Score A?
Score A is where you currently are. GO HORIZONTAL in each function and pick one score as where you currently are. Each sentence in each box represents a number and the 1st sentence represents the 1st number in the box and so on.

What is Score B?
Score B is where you would like to be. GO HORIZONTAL in each function and pick one score as where you currently are. Each sentence in each box represents a number and the 1st sentence represents the 1st number in the box and so on.

How to fill out the Dangers and Opportunities?
Look at each function in the business and identify the dangers that are preventing you from attaining the goal and what are the biggest opportunities that will help you get to those goals.

Where to direct your thinking while utilizing the thinking tool?
Think through each function and fill out what best represents your current score and where you ideally would like to be. When you are thinking about dangers, dangers are something that preventing you from getting forward and pulling you backwards. Biggest opportunities are the opportunities that if you could would help you make the biggest leap in your business towards your ideal score.

Congratulations on completing the exercises and answering the questions for this week. And you have also learned how obstacles can be blessings in disguise. In Week 2, I will teach you how to become a pilot of the time that flies. You need this knowledge to become a businessman of great repute. Before heading off to Week 2, please check out the free resources on the next page. I hope they bring you success.

Useful Resources

QR Code to scan and get all FREE Tools and Resources:

Link from the QR Code:

https://linktr.ee/TheOneYearBreakthrough

Link to all my events:

https://www.eventbrite.com/o/bimal-shah-7943115300

Your Chapter Takeaways

Write out the top 5 key performance indicators of your business that need to be tracked? And how you intend to track them?

1._____
_____
_____

2._____
_____
_____

3._____
_____
_____

4._____
_____
_____

5._____
_____
_____

Time to Celebrate

Before you move to the next chapter, take time to celebrate.

Here are five little ways you can celebrate:

1. Get on Netflix and chill for a while.
2. Go for a short walk.
3. Have a nice dinner with friends.
4. Get a massage to ease out the kinks
5. Draw yourself a hot bath with essential oils to relax.

Week 2

Become the Pilot of the Time That Flies

I have said to myself many times, "Time flies," and continue to say it. It's undoubtedly true. But now I know that when I take charge, I become the pilot and learn how to fly the Plane of Time. It changes everything. It comes with an enormous number of capabilities, resources, and opportunities. It also comes with engine power that is not utilized all the time.

I used to be in the same boat as you and see behind me that time was flying and often felt I was losing control of it. That's when I decided to become a pilot and asked where to find the engine that would make me fly this Airline of Time?

What feeds power into my systems? Is my fuel tank full? Is my plane at full capacity? So many questions . . .

Below, I would like to walk you through a series of mindset exercises, tools, and next steps to help you become the Pilot of Time Airlines.

Do you think you manage your time efficiently? ☐ Y ☐ N

If yes, you have good time-management skills. If you said no to the first time-management question, keep reading to learn how to intentionally develop time-management skills, as they are essential for the success of any business.

Can you do better? ☐ Y ☐ N

If yes, that's great because the biggest room in the world is the room for improvement. Focus on improving your time on a consistent basis. It will help you realize your true potential. Never be satisfied with how you manage your time and what you do with it. Always believe you can do better.

If no, there is a big problem. You have an attitude. Attitude, by the way, is the only word in the English language where the alphabets total up to 100. There is no other word that does that. Your ego is going to be the biggest enemy and destroyer of your own self

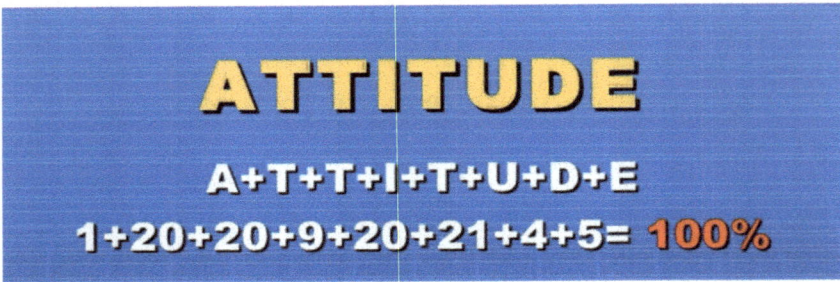

ATTITUDE
A+T+T+I+T+U+D+E
1+20+20+9+20+21+4+5= 100%

What are the top 5 things that are preventing you from managing your time efficiently?

1._____
_____
2._____
_____
3._____
_____
4._____
_____
5._____
_____

You need to think deeply and do a mind-search, so you can discover the things that pose a threat to your time.

What time of the day or week do you allocate to preventing dangers and obstacles to your business?

_____
_____
_____
_____

Dangers and obstacles in business go hand in hand with success. It's important to learn how to prevent dangers and obstacles from harming your business. And that is why it's so helpful to allocate a specific time for solving problems.

Now, before looking at ways to manage our time, let's go over some time-management mistakes you might be making. These mistakes are so common. And most people struggling with their businesses make a couple of them.

1._____
_____
2._____
_____
3._____
_____
4._____
_____
5._____
_____

Did you think deep and hard about this question? Because many of us know and believe we could be managing our time better. But it can be problematic to identify our mistakes. When we manage our time well, we will be more productive in whatever we do. And this leads to a reduction in stress levels. Ultimately, to being happier!

Have you ever had that nagging feeling that you may have forgotten to carry out an important assignment? ☐ Y ☐ N

If you have this feeling, it means, you do not use a To-Do list to be on top of things. To-Do lists help you remember the agenda you have for the day, and which items on the list need to be met so you do not go home, then suddenly slap your hand on your forehead, thinking: *I forgot to submit that proposal today*. But To-Do lists cause stress. So, simply rename the To-Do list "Victories to choose from" and "Outcomes list." If you win more, you work less.

Do you have a Victories list or an Outcomes list? ☐ Y ☐ N

If yes, that's great. If no, separate your true victories from your To-Do list. And then, rename it as "Outcomes" list. The next step is to understand the strategy to using these lists. How will you use a To-Do list for your business?

_____
_____
_____
_____

Using To-Do lists helps you keep a record of what you need to do, and when. The simple trick to using one effectively is to know how to prioritize tasks. You can use an A–D or 1–4 coding system, with A or 1 being high-priority tasks and D or 4 the lowest priority. Additionally, learn to break up big projects into smaller specific, actionable steps.

More important than a To-Do list is a NOT-TO-DO list. Look at your life. Look at some of the things that you consistently do that have led to many of the issues you face or challenges you face. So, you need to prepare a NOT-TO-DO list.

What are the top 5 things you will NOT DO to improve your life?

1._____
_____

2._____
_____

3._____
_____

4._____
_____

5._____
_____

What you don't need to accomplish, and to-do is deeply connected with goal setting.

Do you set personal goals for yourself? ☐ Y ☐ N

If yes, congratulations, you are well on your way to achieving your goals. If no, you need to start setting personal goals for yourself, as in the long run achieving your personal goals will help you achieve your career goals. Everything is linked.
Yes, we have career goals, business goals, but what about your individual growth?

Imagine you were meeting yourself a year from today. You have a magic wand in your hand, and magically, whatever you want to see happen has come true. What would you want to see happen in that year to make you feel happy about your progress?

_____
_____
_____
_____

Where do you see yourself in the next six months, one year, that correlates to how far you will have grown your business?

_____
_____
_____
_____

What are the top 5 things you must do to be where you want in a year?
1._____
_____
2._____
_____
3._____
_____
4._____
_____
5._____
_____

Personal goal setting is key to using your time well, as it gives you a clear vision and destination to work toward. When you can visualize where you want to go, you prioritize your resources and time to achieve your goal.

To take your business to the next level, invest in your self-development. There is a particular level where you can grow your business based on your instincts and natural business sense.

What 5 business-development books have you have read recently?

1._____

_____

2._____

_____

3._____

_____

4._____

_____

5._____

_____

To grow exponentially, you need to learn more. Read more. And interact with those who have done what you seek to achieve. The best leaders are readers. Bill Gates reads daily. You would think a man of his status does not need to develop himself further. But I am not sorry to say, you are wrong.

Do you struggle with distractions when carrying out your tasks? ☐ Y ☐ N

If yes, identify below your distraction triggers and look for how to avoid them. If not, that's great. You will be able to maximize your time and carry out your tasks effectively.
Some people lose vital time to distractions that could have gone to achieving a lot during the work hour. It can be as much as two hours lost to distractions! Just imagine the productivity you could have had with that.

What are your top 5 sources of distractions in your workplace?

1._____
_____

2._____
_____

3._____
_____

4._____
_____

5._____
_____

Daily distractions that take our time away from our business can come in the form of chats, phone calls, colleagues in crisis, or emails. All these can prevent us from achieving our workflow, preventing us from achieving seemingly effortless work that is super satisfying and productive.

What do you think you can do to rid yourself of distractions?

_____
_____
_____
_____

Taking charge of your day involves reducing or minimizing distractions. And managing interruptions to your workflow. For starters, you can make people aware they are disturbing you too much when you are trying to work. When you need to focus, you can stop being available for chats. Additionally, you can learn to work on your concentration. Not getting disturbed easily helps.

Want a system to get rid of interruptions and distractions?

On the next page, you will not only experience a complete system for the same but also experience a process you can use on a recurring basis to become the champion and master pilot of Time Airlines. After you go through the illustration, you will discover how you as a pilot can deal with procrastinations by using them as an advantage and not as a negative.

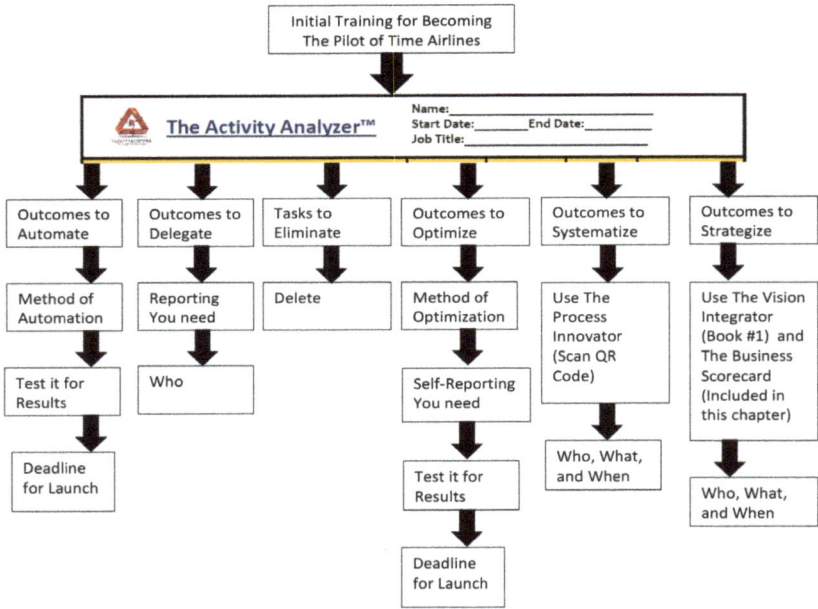

Now that you had the initial training for becoming the Pilot of Time Airlines, let's see how you can use procrastination to your advantage.

Are you guilty of procrastination? ☐ Y ☐ N
If yes, be aware that procrastination is a stealer of time. And time is not something to play with. Once gone, it can never be gotten back. And there's no time to waste when it comes to growing your company. If no, kudos.

Procrastination can be meaningful if done with an eye to priorities. Also, when related to your purpose. But if due to carelessness or forgetfulness, it can hurt you. I have two questions for you. They will help put things in perspective regarding procrastination.

What are the top 10 things you have been consistently procrastinating about that relate to your short-term goal and long-term goals?

1._____

2._____

3._____

4._____

5._____

6._____

7._____

8._____

9._____

10._____

When you're clear what's preventing you from starting, then you move it forward. Most of the time, the issue is getting things started. Things in motion stay in motion. The second question is just below.

What is the biggest element that stands in the way of each of the things you are procrastinating about?

1._____

_____

2._____

_____

3._____

_____

4._____

_____

5._____

_____

6._____

_____

7._____

_____

8._____

_____

9._____

_____

10._____

_____

If there are tasks that you should be working on immediately and you put them off, then you are procrastinating. With procrastination, your mind tells you to put a job off because the task is hard. So, you begin to dread doing it, waiting until the last minute, when it might be too late to complete the task on time.

How do you think you can eliminate procrastination from your business?

_____

_____

_____

_____

A useful strategy for dealing with procrastination, a dangerous time thief, is to break your dreadful big tasks into easy-to-do small bits. And do a little each day. You will be done with the task even before the deadline. And do not put it off till tomorrow; start it now. Just focus on devoting a portion of your time to starting, and before you know it, you are done.

Now you know some of the dangers of time. Think about which ones you may have exposed your business to. And find how—to prevent loss of productivity—you can get rid of the dangers.

What are the top 5 dangers of time to your business?

1._____
_____
2._____
_____
3._____
_____
4._____
_____
5._____
_____

How do you intend to rid yourself of these dangers?

1._____
_____
2._____
_____
3._____
_____
4._____
_____
5._____
_____

To manage your time effectively and avoid the dangers of time loss means understanding the basics of time management. Improving your time-management skills will make you more productive.

Do you plan? ☐ Y ☐ N

If yes, that's great! Efficient planning is needed for the success of any venture. If no, remember, whoever fails to plan plans to fail. So, you need to start planning.

Knowing how to plan is a significant element of good time management. You know it yourself. You know the time of day when you are at your peak. Schedule your most challenging tasks for those intervals. And then schedule your smaller tasks for other times, when though perhaps not at your peak, you can still perform. These tasks will not take much to accomplish.

What time of day are you most productive?

_____

_____

_____

_____

What are your most challenging daily tasks?

1._____

_____

2._____

_____

3._____

_____

4._____

_____

5._____

_____

What are your simpler tasks?

1._____

_____

2._____

_____

3._____
_____

4._____
_____

5._____
_____

So, knowing yourself is key to planning. Also, take time to think about the time of the day when you are at your peak, and when you are not. And then allocate your challenging and simpler tasks for your peak and not-so-peak periods, respectively.

Do you prioritize your tasks? ☐ Y ☐ N

If yes, that's good, as prioritizing will help you identify the major tasks with maximum impact. If no, you need to start prioritizing tasks.

Yes, you can be busy, but what are you busy doing? Are you busy doing tasks that have negligible effect on your business? When you prioritize, you allocate your time to do major tasks that will produce the most impact on your business.

Imagine if you were to cut the word "busy" out of your vocabulary. "Busy" doesn't make you're important or another person is unimportant. Busy-ness is a choice and being productive with your time is a skill. Choose to be productive for yourself and others. Instead of saying, "I don't have time for this," say, "I can't make time for that right now, as my priority is to . . ." When you manage your priorities, you manage your time.

What are the top 5 ways you will manage your time?

1._____
_____

2._____
_____

3._____
_____

4._____
_____

5._____
_____

Think about how to cut out distractions, how to prioritize your tasks, how to defeat procrastination. Think about how to develop yourself, how to improve your concentration.

Do you multitask? ☐ Y ☐ N

If yes, you might want to stop it and learn to focus on a task at a time, as multitasking might make you perform averagely on assigned tasks. In reality, there is no such thing as multitasking. It is either switch-tasking or background-tasking. Switch-tasking is harmful and ineffective, as you are switching from one task to another. And it takes you more time. Background tasking is fine. In that case, you may be, for example, exercising and listening to a podcast at the same time. This is where one task is happening without interfering with your focus on the other.

 If no, that's great. You can learn to further increase the speed at which your complete tasks.

You might think multitasking is a way to get things done faster. Well, it is not. Rather than increasing your productivity, it decreases it. At the end of the day, you will end up with poorly completed projects. And worst-case scenario, you will not be able to finish them.

What do you think is the best alternative to multitasking?

_____

_____

_____

_____

The best alternative to multitasking is giving your complete attention to a single task. Give it your all to avoid mistakes. And when you are done with that task, move on to another one with the same gusto and drive.

Do you reward yourself for a job well done? ☐ Y ☐ N
If yes, this is a nice practice that you already have going; keep it up. If no, start rewarding yourself for a job well done, as it helps boost productivity.

Rewarding yourself when you accomplish tasks can serve as a good motivator to practice proper time management. Learn to give yourself a small reward when you complete a task. You could take a stroll outside or get to return some phone calls.

What are the 5 ways you can motivate yourself after completing a task?

1._____
_____
2._____
_____
3._____
_____
4._____
_____
5._____
_____

Think of things you enjoy doing because only then can they be considered rewards. No, you cannot reward yourself with more work.

Do you keep an inventory of all your activities? ☐ Y ☐ N

If no, keeping an inventory of what you do with your time is essential. If yes, you can compare it to the system I will be sharing later.

When doctors can't figure out what's wrong, they might order a CAT scan or an X-ray. The question is why we don't do the same with our time.

Would you use an activity analyzer for your business? ☐ Y ☐ N

If yes, that's great. If no, why not?
_____
_____

In the pages that follow, I will provide an activity analyzer tool that you can adapt to your business needs and instructions on how to use it.

This productivity tool helps you find out what you do with your time and identify which tasks you enjoy.

	Name: Jane Doe Start Date:_____ End Date:_____ Job Title: Billing Mgr/Front Office Supervisor			
The Activity Analyzer™				
Tasks or Activities (be as specific and Detailed as you can. Please include personal activities or tasks as well if you would like to)	**Average Time**	**No. Times Repeated Weekly**	**Total Weekly Time Taken**	**Circle Love it, Like it, Hate it or Can't (P.T.O for Strategies) (in Excel just delete the icons not applicable)**
Daily Superbills- go through them and sort which are for medical records and which for billing	30 min	x5	2.5 hours	👍
Pull schedules and confirm all encounter were received for all ancillary (allergy,xray, MA visit, CCM, ultrasounds, echo)	5-15 min	x5	25 min ++	👍
Stamp mail	5 min	x5	25 min ++	?
Claim- MSG, Pompano, Hallandale , all ancillary daily claims plus any past claims that were not sign off before	3-4 hours	x5	15 + hours	👍
Back up biller with PPC claims	4-6 hours	when needed		👍
Mail- sort/distribute for medical records/billing/accounting	15 min	x5	1.25 hour	👍
checks/make log for accounting/scan in system/post in system/balance and log (all facility on Friday)	45++ min	x5	3.75 hours ++	👍
Check in money- post patient payment from portal and from the front staff/billing staff, balance and log/give to accounting	30 min	x5	2.5 hours	👍
Electronic- mak log/send to accounting/verify all eob posted correctly if not fix or go find eob and scan and post them/ balance and log on spreadsheet	2 + hours	X5	10+ hours	❤
credit card payments/mailed by patient or insurance company	30 + min	x3	1.5 + hours	👍
Refund requests- request/research/post/ log	30++min	when needed		👍
Work Emails/ Voicemails- Outlook emails/task emails/communicator email/voicemail	depends	everyday multiple x		👍
review /discuss with staff denial management bucket	depends	2x		👍
review rejection bucket/ asst. when needed	depends	5x		👍
work secondary due bucket	depends	5x		👍
review/discuss with staff aging report	depends	monthly		👍
review and work missing encounters	15 min	1x	15 min	👍
asst with billing/staff problems	depends	daily		👍

The Activity Analyzer™	Name: Jane Doe Start Date:_____ End Date:_____ Job Title: Billing Mgr/Front Office Supervisor

Tasks or Activities (be as specific and Detailed as you can. Please include personal activities or tasks as well if you would like to)	Average Time	No. Times Repeated Weekly	Total Weekly Time Taken	Circle Love it, Like it, Hate it or Can't (P.T.O for Strategies) (In Excel just delete the icons not applicable)
Balance end of month with check in, mail, electronic reports give to accounting	2+ hours	monthly		❤️
Appt status report	1 hour	monthly		👍
asst with front staff questions/ problems	depends	daily		👍
Add new CPT codes (mostly custom)	5-10 mins	when needed		👍
Add new insurance and/or update adresses	5-10 mins	when needed		👍
update/change schedules for providers/ancillary	varies	when needed		👍 👎
Look over appt schedules/confirmations/no shows	10-30 min	when can		👍 👎
help with cbd sells	5-10 min	as needed		👍 👎
train/work with staff	depends	as needed		👍
staff evalution 2x a year plus go over with staff	2 hours evaluation/3 hr with staff			👍 👎
Billing issue with emedical	depends on issue	as needed		👍 👎
Help manager (Connie) with answer all emails	depends on #	as needed		👍
payroll approval (tsheet/just works)	1 hour	every other week		👍 👎
Meetings w/managers/department/indiv staff/indiv upper mgmt	1 hour	as needed		👍
Interview new candidates	15-30 min each candidates	when needed		👍 👎
Work with staff to make sure work is completed and not behind	depends	5x		👍

How to Use The Activity Analyzer™ (for the Employee)

Outcome of Proper Utilization of the Tool: Focus on Results, Autonomy, Max Utilization, Proper Work Balance in Company, Time Management, Delegation, Improving Productivity, and much more.

What is the Purpose of the Tool?
Simply put, to discover what you do with your time and what you like, you love, you don't like, or you can't do. Your daily work activities fall into activities that you are incompetent at doing (can't), you are very unique and great at it (Love), you are excellent at it (Like), you are competent but you rather not do it -It irritates you (don't like). Once this tool is filled out, during the workshop, we will first aim to eliminate activities to free up your time (nobody needs to do it!), second is to delegate it and third is to curtail it if we can't delegate or eliminate. On the back side of the tool there are several strategies outlined to help you eliminate, delegate or curtail.

What to fill out?
All progress begins by being completely honest and transparent and you need to be transparent to yourself about your time. Your time is the most valuable resource you have. This is to reflect upon how you currently use your time and what to do about it. So write down all the activities and all the columns and on the symbols you can circle it If you are using PDF or using excel you can change the color of the picture to Green.

Where to direct your thinking while utilizing the thinking tool?
When filling out the activity analyzer, think about every little activity you do with your time. Even if it means you are driving a lot or doing tasks that don't require any human intelligence, write it down. The purpose is to figure out ways to eliminate all of those tasks and activities to bring efficiency, innovation, autonomy, and drive profitability and sales through the roof.

Kudos on completing the exercises and answering the questions for this week, where you have learnt how to manage your time properly and avoid the dangers associated with improper time management. As a result, you will be able to carry out your business tasks and achieve your goals in a timely fashion.

In Week 3, I will teach you about The Good Job Measurer, a tool that will help you revolutionize your business.

P.S.: Before heading off to Week 3, please check out the free resources on the next page, which are provided for your success.

Useful Resources

QR Code to scan and get all FREE Tools and Resources:

Link from the QR Code:

https://linktr.ee/TheOneYearBreakthrough

Link to all my events:

https://www.eventbrite.com/o/bimal-shah-7943115300

Your Chapter Takeaways

What do you believe are the top 5 things you need to do, and the actions you need to take to get them done, to be where you want in one year?

1._____
_____
_____
_____

2._____
_____
_____
_____

3._____
_____
_____
_____

4._____
_____
_____
_____

5._____
_____
_____
_____

Time to Celebrate

Before going straight to the next chapter, make out some time to celebrate.

Here are five little ways you can celebrate:
1. Repeat a celebratory mantra like "I am the creator of my future" or "I am becoming the best version of myself."
2. Get yourself a small gift, like tickets to your favorite show.
3. Listen to your favorite song play in a loop.
4. Bake or order yourself an elaborate dessert.
5. Make your favorite meal

Week 3

The Good Job Measurer

I used to believe that just doing actions and moving forward can help you. But now I know that without tracking and measuring, it won't work. I tried that in the past, and I ended up going in so many directions it was hard to evaluate where I was. I'd rather go a million miles in one direction than a mile in a million directions.

To solve the above, I needed to be able to focus on 10 elements. I need to make sure that my team and I were doing a good job. That's when I created The Good Job Measurer. ™

Below, I walk you through a series of exercises and next steps to help you build The Good Job Measurer system. It will be helpful to you and your team.

Peter Drucker put it quite aptly when he said, "You can't manage what you don't measure. "So, if you do not measure your metrics, how do you know you are improving?

I have my own quote that takes that to a new horizon: "What gets measured and reported daily takes improvement to the next level."

Are you scared of tracking your daily performance? ☐ Y ☐ N

If yes, why? Are you scared of finding out that you are not performing as you should? Well, this is exactly why you should track your daily performance. And work on improving in areas where you are performing poorly. If no, I trust you will keep up the good work.

Do you measure your daily performance? ☐ Y ☐ N

If yes, that's great. You are on the right track. If no, you need to start measuring your daily performance so you can pinpoint areas that need your attention. There are several dangers of not measuring your daily performance. They could include giving up control over performance, not knowing if your strategies are working, not anticipating business dangers and obstacles and preventing them. You see, the list goes on and on.

List the top 5 dangers that you expose your business to by not tracking your daily performance.

1._____
_____
2._____
_____
3._____
_____
4._____
_____
5._____
_____

You might wonder about how to build a customized system of tracking and accountability. Below is an illustration of the same:

Building a Customized Daily Tracking and Accountability System

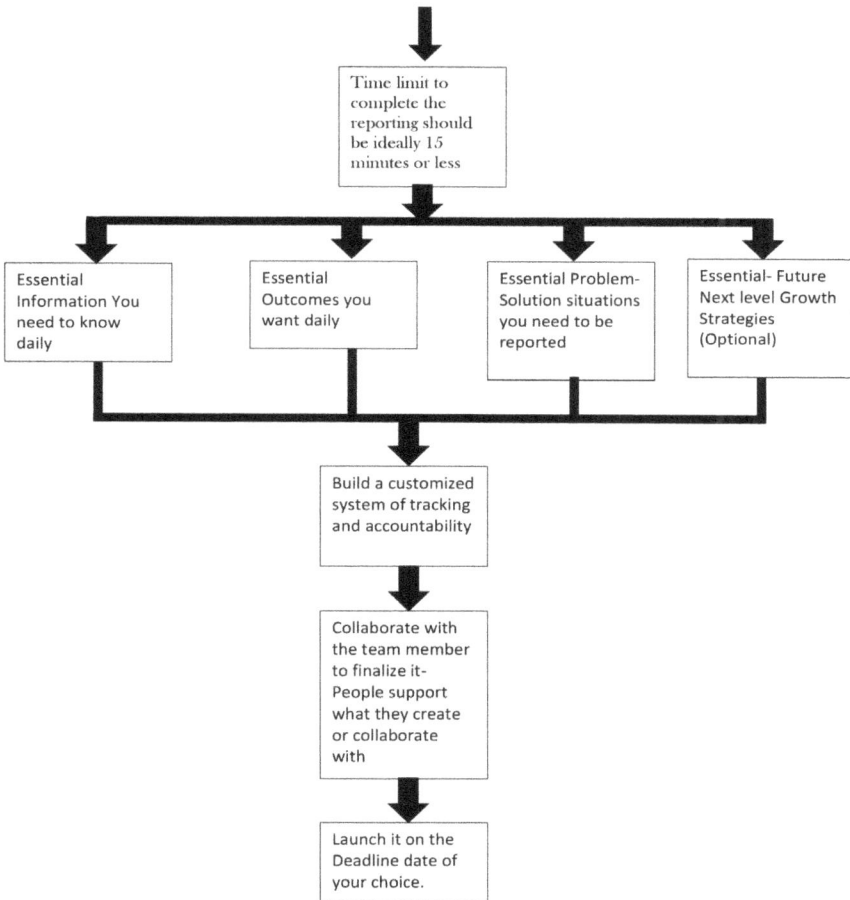

```
┌─────────────────┐
│ Time limit to   │
│ complete the    │
│ reporting should│
│ be ideally 15   │
│ minutes or less │
└─────────────────┘
```

Essential Information You need to know daily	Essential Outcomes you want daily	Essential Problem-Solution situations you need to be reported	Essential- Future Next level Growth Strategies (Optional)

```
┌─────────────────┐
│ Build a customized│
│ system of tracking│
│ and accountability│
└─────────────────┘

┌─────────────────┐
│ Collaborate with │
│ the team member  │
│ to finalize it-  │
│ People support   │
│ what they create │
│ or collaborate   │
│ with             │
└─────────────────┘

┌─────────────────┐
│ Launch it on the │
│ Deadline date of │
│ your choice.     │
└─────────────────┘
```

Now that you have learned how to build a customized system, let's understand the consequences of not doing it.

Let's look at some of the dangers. You will see how you're causing your business more harm than good if you are not using your key performance indicators.

Do you know that you're doing no better than guesswork when you don't track your performance? ☐ Y ☐ N

If yes, then why would you want to keep on guessing when you can work with exact figures? If no, well now you know; you've been doing guesswork, and it's time to do something about it.

How do you take the guesswork out of your business performance?

_____

_____

_____

_____

For an organization, meeting its goal it is the result of decisions and actions. And in our complex business world, many factors will affect your business. You need to make informed decisions to continue with what is working and stop what is not working. And this can be accomplished if you track your daily progress.

How do you know that your business strategies are working or not working as the case may be?

_____

_____

_____

_____

Anyone can just stand up and say that a strategy worked. And how can you disprove the statement without measurements? Measurements give precise information, objectively. They show what we can't notice quickly: the little changes, a gradual and steady change, or no change at all. And we need to be aware of these changes, whether small or not, to know if a given strategy is working.

Do you know that without measurements, your business will just be mediocre? ☐ Y ☐ N

If yes, then I hope you are measuring your performance. If no, why would you want to be mediocre when you can be excellent? Always measure your performance.

Yes, without measurements, your business will be mediocre at best. Because without accurate performance measures, you and your teammates will miss out on opportunities to improve performance further.

How can you improve your business performance?

_____
_____
_____
_____

Suppose everything seems to be performing well, and no one is measuring any key performance metrics. In that case, you will not have much leverage to improve your business performance, as your business can be doing better, but you simply don't know.
How do you anticipate and prevent dangers and obstacles in your business?

_____
_____
_____
_____

Prediction is an integral part of business success. You will be able to predict when something is about to go wrong. And you can seek ways to avoid it. However, a prediction is not possible without measurements. Without measurements, you will end up cleaning up a mess that could have easily been prevented.

Knowing what you know now about the dangers of not tracking your performance, how do you intend to start tracking your daily progress?

1._____
_____

2._____

_____

3._____

_____

4._____

_____

5._____

_____

How do you measure your daily job performance or performance of your team members?

_____

_____

_____

_____

I have created The Good Job Measurer to measure and keep track of important job metrics and activities. With this business-productivity tool, you can track your most valuable business activities and important job metrics and activities.

Would you invest in a measurement tool for your business? ☐ Y ☐ N

If yes, that's a good business decision. If no, read on to find out why you need one.

Organizations invest a lot of resources in performance-management related activities. The large global company Deloitte underwent a revamp. They discovered 65,000 employees spent about 2 million hours a year holding meetings. Some spent their time completing forms and analyzing ratings. Yet many business owners and employees were not happy with their performance. The quality and effectiveness were not there.[2]
Are you dissatisfied with your performance measurements? ☐ Y ☐ N

So, if you are dissatisfied with your performance measurements, you need to use The Good Job Measurer tool. On the next page is a sample of The Good Job Measurer that you can adapt to suit your business needs and instructions on how to use it efficiently.

The "Good Job" Measurer™

Target Ideal Weekly Score_____

No.	What are the Most Valuable Activities?	How will KPI be measured? Result	Score (1-10)
1	ACCOMMODATE CLIENT'S WORK HOURS SCHEDULING BY BEING AVAILABLE AND PROVIDING SUPERVISION AT JOB SITE DURING WEEKENDS, EVENINGS, HOLIDAYS OR AT ANY TIME	INCREASES SCHEDULING VERSATILITY. INCREASES CLIENT SATISFACTION. INCREASES COMPANY REVENUE.	
2	ADVANCE SCHEDULING AND COORDINATION WITH SUBCONTRACTORS OF REQUIRED MANPOWER AND MATERIAL NEEDS TO MEET SCHEDULE.	KEEPS CLIENT HAPPY BY MEETING OR EXCEEDING PROJECT SCHEDULE. ENSURES CONTINUOUS WORK FLOW BY MINIMIZING DELAYS. ALLOWS SUBCONTRACTORS TO SCHEDULE RESOURCES IN ADVANCE.	
3	JOB SITE CLEANLINESS.	KEEPS CLIENT ND SUBCONTRACTORS HAPPY. INCREASES PRODUCTIVITY. REDUCES RISK.	
4	HIGH PERCENTAGE OF APPROVED INSPECTIONS FROM GOVERNING AUTHORITIES.	MINIMIZES DELAYS	
5	THROUGHOUT THE DAY MONITOR THAT WORK IS PERFORMED SAFELY, IN COMPLIACE WITH DRAWING SPECS, MATERIALS AND		
	Total		

| Position: | SUPERINTENDENT | | | | |

| Prepared By: JOHN DOE Date: 06/10/2021 | | | | | |

Performance Day Scores			Preparation Day Scores			Total for the Week -->
Day___	Day ___	Day ___	Day___	Day ___	Day___	

How to Use The Good Job Measurer™

Outcome of the Tool: Autonomy and Max Utilization of the Team.

What is the Purpose of the Tool?
To discover the five to ten most valuable activities that each of your team members can do in an ideal environment to yield the highest results for the pay and benefits.

What to fill out?
Only the top portion with your name and details and the two columns highlighted in Yellow. The rest of the sections will be trained on how to utilize in the workshops.

Where to direct your thinking while utilizing the thinking tool?
When filling out the most valuable activity, think about the activities that you have the unique ability to do it better than anyone else and that you can deliver the best results. When filling out the ideal results, think about what would be the highest result for the company on the activity you are doing and what would be the ideal time frame if applicable.

High five on completing the exercises and answering the questions in this week, as you have learned about the importance of measuring work done, and you have been equipped with a tool for it. Next week, I will teach you about understanding the process of getting stuck. This will help you get out of difficult situations. Before heading off to next week, please check out the free resources on the next page, as they are sure to enhance your success.

Useful Resources

QR Code to scan and get all FREE Tools and Resources:

Link from the QR Code:

https://linktr.ee/TheOneYearBreakthrough

Link to all my events:

https://www.eventbrite.com/o/bimal-shah-7943115300

Your Chapter Takeaways

How will you track the job progress and measure the performance of everyone on the team, including yourself?

Time to Celebrate
Before going to the next chapter, take time to celebrate.

Here are five small and simple ways you can celebrate:
1. Buy yourself ice cream.
2. Go on date night with your partner.
3. Do yoga.
4. Meditate.
5. Plan a meetup with friends.

Week 4

Understanding the Process of Getting Stuck

I have discovered myself many times in a place where I am stuck. Now that I understand the process of getting stuck. It helps me get unstuck faster and more efficiently than anything else.

I used to get stuck in many elements in my business. And I started wondering why this was happening to me repeatedly. That's when I realized that getting stuck is a process. It happens systematically to everyone. So, I started digging, and the first step I took was to walk backward when I was thinking. I kept asking myself: What's the benefit of walking backward? Then I took twenty steps backward and looked ahead. What I saw was a runway!! That's when the light bulb struck. I saw that obstacles, when they push you backward, give you the runway to run up to a point. You either leap high or leap far. Ignoring obstacles is a big danger because they are an opportunity to build that runway.

Below, I would like to walk you through a series of questions, exercises, tools. Next, I focus on examining the process of getting stuck. And help you build the runway to leap high or leap far or fly.

What are the top 5 factors that push your business backward?

1._____

_____

2._____

_____

3._____

_____

4._____

_____

5._____

_____

Being able to eliminate dangers and obstacles makes the path to success super easy. So, let's identify and overcome the dangers and obstacles.

What 5 ways can you eliminate your previously identified dangers and obstacles?

1._____

_____

2._____

_____

3._____

_____

4._____

_____

5._____

_____

Everyone will face certain dangers and obstacles at one point or the other. However, the way you tackle these matters will determine whether you get burnt or overcome the dangers and obstacles unscathed.

What are the top 5 problems your business is facing now?

1._____
_____

2._____
_____

3._____
_____

4._____
_____

5._____
_____

A successful entrepreneur learns how to jump over dangers and obstacles while running towards the desired goal.

How do you intend to solve those 5 problems?
1._____
_____

2._____
_____

3._____
_____

4._____
_____

5._____
_____

Want to put out the biggest fires in your business? See the next page . . .

Building An Army of Fire Extinguishers in Your Business

Putting Our Fires Regularly?

```
                    Biggest Reasons Fires
                    Happen Regularly
```

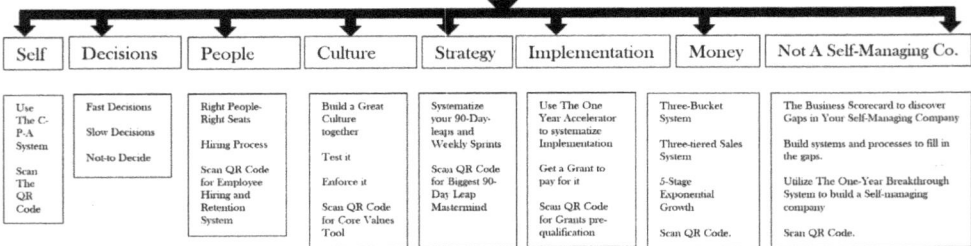

Self	Decisions	People	Culture	Strategy	Implementation	Money	Not A Self-Managing Co.
Use The C-P-A System Scan The QR Code	Fast Decisions Slow Decisions Not-to Decide	Right People-Right Seats Hiring Process Scan QR Code for Employee Hiring and Retention System	Build a Great Culture together Test it Enforce it Scan QR Code for Core Values Tool	Systematize your 90-Day-leaps and Weekly Sprints Scan QR Code for Biggest 90-Day Leap Mastermind	Use The One Year Accelerator to systematize Implementation Get a Grant to pay for it Scan QR Code for Grants pre-qualification	Three-Bucket System Three-tiered Sales System 5-Stage Exponential Growth Scan QR Code.	The Business Scorecard to discover Gaps in Your Self-Managing Company Build systems and processes to fill in the gaps. Utilize The One-Year Breakthrough System to build a Self-managing company Scan QR Code.

Store all the Fire Extinguishers in a place that is safe and easily accessible by whoever needs to access it.

Know that 99.99 percent of obstacles and dangers can be avoided because they stem from habitual mistakes, unmanaged emotions, and ingrained habits.

Habits can change right away or can take a long time to change, depending on how rooted we are in them. The most immediate way to look at changing habits is to see what triggers you for a specific habit. Once you understand, you can either remove the triggers outright or swap them for something else associated with that habit. For example, you may have a habit of snacking occasionally while you work. Hence, causing you to be overweight and unhealthy. Instead, think of your snack as a short walk to get fresh air; consider walking as food for your body and your mind.

What do you think will happen to you or your business if your obstacles and dangers are left unattended?

_____
_____
_____
_____

Obstacles and dangers are emotional thieves in your life. If you don't make the effort to correct them, they will sap your mental energy. They will steal your focus and prevent you from accomplishing your goals.

Now, let's dive into strategies that will help you overcome your biggest dangers and challenges.

Do you listen to your gut when it concerns people? ☐ Y ☐ N

If yes, that's good. Learning to trust your intuition can save you from avoidable problems. If no, you need to start.

We all possess this in-built radar that warns us of an impending danger or obstacle when it concerns people. However, many times most of us choose to ignore it. And research has shown that one in four startups fail due to managerial incompetence.

Evaluate your teammates. Are they competent to handle the tasks given to them? ☐ Y ☐ N

If no, can their competencies be improved? ☐ Y ☐ N

If yes, how do you go about getting them to improve their competencies?

_____
_____
_____
_____

And, if their competencies cannot be improved, then they are not a good fit for your organization.

Another obstacle to business success is emotional pricing.

Do you fall into the pit of letting your emotions dictate the price you charge for your products? ☐ Y ☐ N

If yes, you need to stop letting your emotions dictate the price. If no, congratulations, you have learnt to charge according to the value you are putting out there.

Many entrepreneurs don't have the right pricing for their goods and services. So, sometimes their emotions dictate how much they charge. For instance, we can be afraid of losing a sale. Hence, we charge little, leading to a continuous lowering of our profit margin. This is dangerous, creating a big obstacle down the road.

What can you do to combat emotional pricing?

_____
_____
_____
_____

Learn to set prices with your head and not your heart. You should know your costs. Study and observe your competition; regularly evaluate your prices. You can also ask your customers for feedback regarding your pricing. Most will be happy to help. And even give you some valuable insights concerning your business niche. All the above strategies given are geared to lead you towards rational pricing.

Knowing what you know now, what will be your top 5 strategies to combat emotional pricing?

1._____
_____
2._____
_____
3._____
_____
4._____
_____
5._____
_____

As entrepreneurs, we tend to fall so in love with our products that we find it hard to let go of what is not working. Have you forgotten that to sustain success, one must be willing to let go of things that are no longer successful?

Do you abandon what is not working in your business? ☐ Y ☐ N

If yes, that's great. Of course, it might be hard to abandon practices you are accustomed to. But it is important to know when something has outlived its usefulness. It will help the success of any business. If no, you need to learn to cut out things that are no longer working, so they don't drag your business down.

Knowing what you know now, from Week 3, how do you intend to find out what is working or not working in your business?

_____
_____
_____
_____

You must act fast when evaluating what is not working. And you must have the courage to cut it out of your business. Else, it poses a significant danger and obstacle to your business.

Every entrepreneur should be open to learning new strategies.
Are you open to innovation and learning new strategies? ☐ Y ☐ N

If yes, that's awesome! You are on the right track to taking your business to the next level. Innovation and taking risks are necessary skills for the growth of any business in this era. If no, you need to start being innovative, as it is vital to having a successful business.

Sometimes, as an entrepreneur, you can cling to outdated ways of doing business. Because it is what you know how to do best. It is working. This is a slippery slope to stagnancy and getting overtaken by the competition. For example, you can choose to rely on outbound marketing tactics. And refuse to consider inbound marketing value. Therefore, closing the door to other customers.

The majority of the time, either you are in the wrong market or you have the wrong message. The key is being in the right market with the right message. Take time to select the niche market. Building the right message can solve many of your problems. Identifying new and proven to work strategies to be in the right market with the right message is the next step.

Knowing what you know now, I want you to think deeply and identify the top 5 ways that you might be hindering your business by refusing to adopt new and proven work strategies.

1._____

_____

2._____

_____

3._____

_____

4._____

_____

5._____

_____

Now you have identified ways that you have been hurting your business by refusing to innovate with time. How do you intend to overcome this obstacle to your business?

1._____
_____
2._____
_____
3._____
_____
4._____
_____
5._____
_____

Thumbs up on completing the exercises and answering the questions in this book. It has equipped you with tools and knowledge to help you eliminate dangers and obstacles from your business. So, it's an onwards journey to the top of your industry for you. Before putting down this book, please check out the free resources on the next page; they are provided for your tremendous growth and success.

Useful Resources

QR Code to scan and get all FREE Tools and Resources:

Link from the QR Code:

https://linktr.ee/TheOneYearBreakthrough

Link to all my events:

https://www.eventbrite.com/o/bimal-shah-7943115300

Your Chapter Takeaways

With what you have learnt from this chapter, how do you intend to take your business to the next level?

Time to celebrate
Kudos on finishing book 3. Before going to book 4, take time to celebrate.

Here are five simple small ways you can celebrate:
1. Order takeouts for the family and have a restful evening.
2. Get on video call with extended family.
3. Bake your favorite dessert.
4. Go for a pedicure.
5. Dance, dance, dance.

Doubling Your Business and Taking Over Your Industry in a Year!

Hidden Insights from this Book

Below, I have provided proven uncharted bottom-line insights from this book to double your business and rise in your industry in a year:

1. Obstacles Are a Blessing in Disguise:
Make three columns on a page- Obstacles, Strategies that overcome the obstacles and deliver the highest payoff, and who needs to do what by when. Do this exercise on a blank page as often as possible, and you will see your business double and soar. You can use the same exercise to become "the only one" in your industry.

2. Become the Pilot of the Time That Flies:
To manage your time better, it is very important to get a sound sleep. The most important alarm is not your wake-up alarm, but your winding-down alarm. Please keep an alarm for when you need to stop everything and just start preparing to go to bed. We all need a minimum of 7 hours of sleep and plan your winding-down alarm accordingly. Trust me, you will double your results and output doing that.

3. The Good Job Measurer:
To double your business, have The Good Job Measurer filled out by everyone in your team including your top executives and team members and you also fill out for the ones you directly manage. Have your team members do the same for the team members they manage. You will be shockingly surprised at the mismatch. It will open your eyes and help you scale your business and become unique.

4. Understanding the Process of Getting Stuck:
You get stuck in business by repetitive ignorance. So, the first time you face any problem that repeats itself and seems very small or ok, pay attention to it. It can get bigger and bigger and force you to get stuck. Make changes and improvements the moment you see it. This will double your business in a year.

DON'T FORGET

Join The Pioneers Club for FREE!

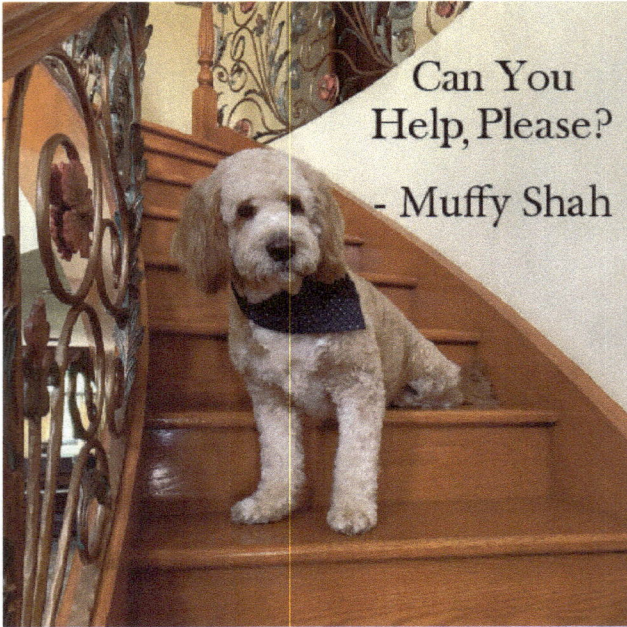

Can You
Help, Please?

- Muffy Shah

Thank You for Reading My Book!

I really appreciate your reading my book!

I would love it if you can give me an honest review.
I need your input to make the next version and my future books better.

Please leave me a helpful 5-Star review on Amazon, letting me know
what you thought!

Thank you so much!

—Bimal Shah

Please don't forget to check out the next book that will assist you in eliminating your biggest dangers and obstacles.

This is the next step in the sequence of steps to Becoming a Pioneer by achieving your three-year goal in one year.

See you in book 4!

DON'T FORGET

Join The Pioneers Club for FREE!

WHAT IS THE PIONEER CLUB FOR A BUCK?

- Buy the book for a Buck and you join the club
- Meet and network with other Pioneers
- Walk away with great results at the club meeting
- Complete the exercises in the book
- FREE Tools and Resources
- Win an Invitation to the Mastermind ($495 Value)
- Provide a great review on Amazon

https://bit.ly/ThePioneersClub

With each book, you are Eligible to Join the Club Meeting for FREE

Connect with Pioneers around the World—Every Month. With the book purchase, you are a member. No strings attached.

Connect with Me and walk away with personalized insights for you in the Club meeting held every month.

Get Your FREE Membership at:

https://bit.ly/ThePioneersClub

Conclusion

I strongly suggest you research modern, tried-and-tested techniques for businesses. I mean those techniques that have taken businesses to the next level. And think of how you can include them as part of your business growth strategy.

Not sure how to go about the research? You can start by interacting with your business mentors. Reach out to those who have gone through the path you are currently treading. Enrich yourself from their pool of knowledge and experience; glean insights from them.

Also, study your competitors. Look at what they are doing. Ask what is working for them and look for ways to improve on your competitors' strategies in order to overtake them and dominate the marketplace. Remember, the goal is to be ahead of your competition.

Incorporate all the tips and insights in this workbook. It will help you eliminate your biggest dangers and obstacles. See you in book 4.

About the Author

Bimal Shah is an accomplished Senior Executive, Entrepreneur, Advisor, Coach, and Results Leader with more than twenty years of success in the financial-services industry. Leveraging extensive experience in growth, entrepreneurship, talent development, financial reporting systems, profitability systems, and processes to scale, he is an asset for companies spanning various industries, sizes, and stages of growth that are seeking expert assistance in bringing their business to the next level. His broad areas of expertise include executive coaching, strategic planning, operations management, scaling, and growth.

As a breakthrough coach, Bimal has successfully helped companies generate growth of more than 50 percent in a year and has taken twenty-six companies to exponential growth in a year. Through his unique hiring process technique, he has helped dozens of companies hire highly qualified C-Level employees. He has worked with more than fifty companies in providing coaching and financial consulting services across an array of industries, including manufacturing, distribution, home health care, communications industry, security systems, and professional services. His unique Coaching-Planning-Accountability system has generated favorable results in record time for CEOs, reducing their working hours, in six months, by 35 percent.

As a result, CEOs see exponential company growth within a year's time, can hire smart and productive team members at all levels within a few months, and receive the tools to develop effective "out of the box" marketing strategies.

Bimal is also the founder of Rajparth Advisory Group (2005), which provides financial consulting services to entrepreneurs.

From 1996 to 2005, prior to founding Rajparth Group, he worked as an independent advisor through Northwestern and New York Life, helping more than 1000 families preserve their assets, reduce their taxes, increase their income, and create everlasting legacies.

During his tenure, he was awarded the highest honor in the industry, The Million Dollar Round Table—Top of the Table Award for six years in a row and Global Corporate Award for Best Life Insurance Agent in the Asian Indian Community.

Bimal has also authored and published *The Daily Happiness Multiplier*, available on Amazon and in bookstores throughout North America. His unique "Success Deck" consists of 52 Workshop Videos and Tools to positively impact anyone's personal and professional life with a single tool each week for 52 weeks. Bimal earned his Bachelor of Commerce in Economics from the University of Mumbai and his Bachelor of Science in Advertising from the University of Florida. He holds a Chartered Financial Consultant, Chartered Life Underwriter, and Certified Advisor in Senior Living from the American College at Bryn Mawr, Pennsylvania.

Some Accolades for Bimal's Work

"Bimal is the big picture guy and he takes us really deep. I might concentrate on one idea that I think is the greatest idea in this world, and Bimal will come back with making us think 10 times bigger and he's got this amazing ability to see opportunity. He lays out a great plan to get to where you want to go and makes it just so attainable. Every entrepreneur with big goals should consider hiring
Bimal and if I could have Bimal in my pocket and carry him around at all times that would be great."
— Mike Barnhill, Managing Partner, Specialist ID

"Before, I was working 70-80 hours a week. Now it is down to 45-55 hours a week. The personal impact of his coaching has allowed me to spend more time with my family. The financial impact has been priceless because of the time saved. If you are struggling, consider hiring Bimal. His books and coaching have helped me plan and organize where I want the business to go. Bimal has also taught me to push my limits and think about things more in detail on why I am doing this."
—Reginald Andre, CEO, Ark Solvers, Inc.

"Bimal's books and workshops have further reinforced and enhanced some aspects of my leadership, in that he has brought on a fresh perspective to my role as a leader of the company. In addition to Bimal being a very engaging and energetic personality, he also has an open-minded and unique perspective to making learning a fun-filled experience for my staff, which then adds immeasurable value to my company."

—Terry Sgamatto, Managing Regional Director, Seeman Holtz

"I recently took a leap of faith . . . one that required a consistent amount of convincing myself out of a scarcity mindset and making an investment. It has just been a few weeks and I am very happy with the results of my decision. Under the advisement of Bimal, I have had to make some drastic decisions in my company but have to say overall, even though some were painful, they have all been results-driven and not emotional. I truly appreciate all that Bimal has helped me create in the first few weeks and cannot wait to see what comes next."

—Sarah Martin, CEO, Experience Epic, LLC

Notes

1   "2022 Is Seeing a Surge in Entrepreneurship," https://natural-zing.com/blogs/launching-a-health-and-wellness-biz/2022-is-seeing-a-sur-ge-in-entrepreneurship#:~:text=In%202019%2C%20the%20failure%20rate,'t%20succeed%2C%20try%20again.

2   Marcus Buckingham and Ashley Goodall, "Reinventing Perfor-mance Management," https://hbr.org/2015/04/reinventing-performan-ce-management.